Awaking my Sleeping Heart

TABLE OF CONTENTS

Warmth

The glow of your love
Cages my fears
Allowing me to walk barefoot
On the snow
Protecting me from the chill
Of unknown demons
Seeking my soul
To quench their hunger
For the obsolete.

I fall into your
Consoling arms.
You smile down
At me, as I
Glance back up at my
Sense of home.

We begin to laugh
Ourselves into our
Alternate Universe.
The warmth of
The other person's joy
Keeping our hearts
Beating in perfect rhythm.

I look out the window
To see the vibrant
harmony of colors
make up the sunset.
Signaling the warmth
Leaving for the night
You grab me, and we melt
more into each other
Fully content with doing
Whatever it takes to
Keep the glow alive
As we drift mindlessly
to rest.

Remedy

A dark shadow hangs over me…
Piercing my joy, and bruising my
fragile heart.
Days are longer to live
Harder to rationalize
My own love feels foreign,
the touch from my pillow is
The only comfort I know.

Somewhere in my journey,
You found me
Awake but not alive.
You saw my tears for what they were
You hugged life back into my cold
dark heart,
And put hope into the most desolate
Parts of me.

Skeptical but intrigued
I fell into you.
I lived In your world
of light, and love.
My hopeless brain wandering into
The unknown feeling of security.

Feeling safe and oblivious I didn't feel you
slipping away,
Until you were already gone.
As my world uncontrollably darkened
I realized
You were the only remedy I ever knew.

Sleep

I blissfully sleep in a field of lost
love.
Unconscious, as to not see the
horror of reality
Peacefully numb
Numbingly at peace.

The dark cloud tries to pierce
through my dreams,
I toss and turn
Punching the air
And for a second….
I almost remember
you.

Fear pulls me back into a deep rem
And I escape your grasp
Blissfully sleeping
Peacefully numb
So please…
don't wake me.

Denial

They told me you were dangerous.
I ran home to you
and shuttered all the windows
"It's okay" I assured you,
they can't sever through our reality here.

I remember your words,
and how they paralyzed me.
You did not mean them though
I can see your intentions
Through the soft pupils
Staring back at me eagerly
Lost, looking for direction
You're safe here.

We talk all night until
The soft glow of the fire
Sends us off to sleep.
Peacefully at rest,
Knowing everything is okay.

A noise wakes me up
I turn over to you,
You're crying,
I go to console you
But something stops me.
For some reason
Your presence has become unsettling.

I convince myself it's in my head
And I go over to provide comfort,
That's when you up look at me, and
I instantly stop in my tracks.
Those aren't the soft eyes I remember so well.
The ones I've seen so many times,
The ones that feel like home.
These are dark eyes
Ones with malice.
And then it happens,
You pull out the sharpest of knives
And pierce me right in my stomach.

You pull it out slowly,
And as the life leaves my body
My eyes lock with yours
One final time.
As they begin to slowly close,
And I slip away
my last thought
Is I'd rather be dead,
then ever believe you were
dangerous like they said.

Mourning

Good morning,
I'm in mourning.
White roses on the grave
Of the one I once knew.
Love spilled all over the floor,
Wiped dry with scripture.

Good morning,
I'm in mourning.
Staring blankly at
Your life filled body
Confused at what my
eyes are seeing.
The voice of comfort
That was once so healing
Has now obliterated me
Into a small glass of nothing.

Good morning,
I'm in mourning.
Salty tears keep me
Hydrated from my thoughts
Blankets keep me warm
from the chill of your trauma,
Now my trauma,
Which you so kindly let me inherit.

Good morning,
I'm in mourning.
Standing as still as a statue
Frozen in time
Too scared to move
Too scared of what change will
come next
Content with watching life go by
On the big screen.

So Good morning,
I'm in mourning.
Mourning you,
And everything that used to be true.

Time

Those sacred tender moments
Where time completely halts
Around you
Nothing you once knew
Feels real anymore.
All of your precious dreams
No longer feel obtainable.

The tears on your cheek seem
To fall in slow motion,
Even when you're crying so hard
You cannot breathe.

Completely consumed by silence,
because there is nothing worth
hearing,
the adult in you reverts
back to an innocent helpless child.

You reach up longing for comfort.
This isn't the life you agreed to
join,
This wasn't the experience you
were promised.

But there is no one,
There is nothing,
Just reality to feel
In slow motion.
Because that's where
pain
is most
Venomous.

Serenity

Back and forth we go
Like a wave
So full of wonder and passion
I pause to take you in
Your beauty is crippling
But so are we

People fear the complex
But for me it's intriguing
We are like a wave
So peaceful and serene
Spreading our love
The best way we know how
But waves eventually crash
And so will we

Yours eyes look angry
So I soften mine
Your yells are loud
So I calm my voice
I watch you,
And mirror your needs
That is love I tell myself
That is love.

Your anger is soothing
Your passion validating
Through the war
I am at peace
Rocking back and forth
Full of innocence
As the wave of you
Crashes over me.

Resentment

My body
My home
the lights inside are dim
My breath is narrow
unliberated
Shackled to pain
My thoughts race against themselves
I cannot sleep unless I'm tired of feeling.

How could I feel this way?
In my own body
My home
The only escape I ever known
How could you make me feel this way?
When you told me you loved me
When our passion and intimacy dipped past the
physical and danced into the canvas
painting the masterpieces that is us.
I thought we became one.
We faught for our freedom,
You were the soilder by my side
But you gave up on us
You gave up on me.

In my body
In my home
I think about you
I wonder why the promises
You had me make
were never reciprocated
I wonder if you're happy with
My replacement, really the
replacement of the pain
You felt losing me?
I wonder if you think about
The pain I feel?
The nights I lied awake and wondered.

I go back and forth in my mind
Wanting you to come back home to me,
And never wanting to see you again
Blaming you for the pain I feel,
And telling myself it's not your fault
Resenting you,
and trying to find
Some type of
understanding and peace.

Understanding

Tossing, turning, yearning
Fighting to live the truth
Of unconditional love that I
Preach so much
My skin still on fire
I melt into my tear soaked bed
Drowning in the memories of you
I catch my breath to whisper one
Little word
"Why, my love?"

It's okay my love
I've been better these days
More awake
I see us for what we were
I cherish our moments and memories
More than you know
My sadness now a distant cousin
I'm slowly able to dissect the
story of us.

My love,
I'm confused.
I walked on burning stones
Drowned in dangerous waters
Slept on stone
Cried
Bleed
Screamed
And yet my quest for understanding
Has left me more bruised than you did.

My love
I've been unfair
Of course you loved me
And you tried your best
Our paths were just not destined
even though we longed, and shapeshifted
it wasn't enough.
I haven't been conscious of your pain
I haven't wished for your happiness
For that I'm deeply sorry
And also, I forgive you.

Time Pt.2

The curse of time
Helped foster an environment
Of growth and healing
The distance of time
It took to come to a
Harsh painful understanding
Is like running around the world
Twice.

The rollercoaster of emotions
How much pain I felt at any given moment
fluctuated
But time picked me up off the ground
The hands on the clock wrapping
Around me in a nurturing bear hug
I felt my heart starting to be open to love again
I stopped using sleep as a way to
evade reality.

Just when I thought I reached homeostasis
the song of us blasted through the speakers
…. I completely freeze
All the time it took to heal me
Suddenly vanishes and I'm left
There wounds open
Remembering you

But time doesn't abandon you
It's consistent
It doesn't get hurt when you try to avoid it
It doesn't stop allowing you to heal
It reminds you that your life
Is ahead of you not behind
You have all the time in the world

The end

About the Author

Kirby Maze is an avid reader and writer. Taking after his Mom who is a published author. In high school, he won the undergraduate award for excellence in English, and was the President of poetry club. Teaching his classmates, and anyone who will listen, the power of words on paper.